CANDY

SEWANEE POETRY

Wyatt Prunty and Leigh Anne Couch, Series Editors

DAN ALBERGOTTI

CANDY

POEMS

Louisiana State University Press
Baton Rouge

Published by Louisiana State University Press
lsupress.org

LSU Press Paperback Original

DESIGNER: Barbara Neely Bourgoyne
TYPEFACES: Adobe Text Pro, text; Gotham, display

Cover illustration courtesy AdobeStock/Kacpura.

LIBRARY OF CONGRESS CATALOGING-IN-PUBLICATION DATA
Names: Albergotti, Dan, author.
Title: Candy : poems / Dan Albergotti.
Description: Baton Rouge : Louisiana State University Press, 2024. |
    Series: Sewanee poetry
Identifiers: LCCN 2024009560 (print) | LCCN 2024009561 (ebook) |
    ISBN 978-0-8071-8254-3 (paperback) | ISBN 978-0-8071-8283-3 (epub) |
    ISBN 978-0-8071-8284-0 (pdf)
Subjects: LCGFT: Poetry.
Classification: LCC PS3601.L3343 C36 2024 (print) | LCC PS3601.L3343
    (ebook) | DDC 811/.6—dc23/eng/20240304
LC record available at https://lccn.loc.gov/2024009560
LC ebook record available at https://lccn.loc.gov/2024009561

CONTENTS

III

CANDY

Kick in the Jaw

Sometimes the zebra wins. And the sound
of the savanna goes on—birdsong, frog croak,

beetle chitter, snort and grunt of a warthog,
hard panting of the cheetah after chase—

as the lion walks slowly away, bleeding
from the mouth, staring ahead, looking for a place

to rest and await a slow starvation. Sometimes
the savanna's ambient song is interrupted

by a sharp crack that sounds like a gunshot,
the zebra's kick finding the lion's jaw.

Some stories get rewritten. Sometimes
the lion dies. Always the sound goes on.

The Father

Imagine the father as a gardener who plants
and harvests only at night. Imagine the son
and daughter told to make other of themselves.
Imagine an edict against understanding edicts.
Imagine a sibilant song that swims in the soil
like a leviathan. Imagine piercing the skin.
Imagine chewing fennel, an earthy taste of sweet
bitterness, the touching of toes to lips. Imagine
there's no heaven, only a gated garden of bush
and tree and grass and flower and grove and growth
and beast and bawling child. Imagine losing all that.
Imagine a father drinking from a dark cistern of tears.

The Servant's Ear

The servant's ear has fallen to the ground
and hears now, from its nest of bloody grass,
the squabbling of the savior and his men.

And hears, of course, the screaming from the head
that was its home just two seconds ago
and orders hissed by the arresting priest,

then rustling of a processional gait—
the march to make the prisoner face the law—
and silver pieces jingling in a sack.

The footsteps fade. There's not another sound
for hours as history begins to pass
this simple, severed organ without sin.

It will lie for decades on its green bed,
listening to crickets, the occasional crow.
Out of the story, it still has at least

a half a century, maybe more, to wait
for Luke to lift it into myth, to draw
it up and, with his pen, to put it back.

The Fall of a Turtle

Apparently you can survive three battles
in the era of the phalanx, write eighty-two tragedies,
win prizes, strut around in your laurel crown
bathing in everyone's unremitting praise,
and still manage to die at sixty-seven in a Sicilian field
from being conked on the head by a turtle
dropped from the talons of a bearded vulture
just looking to break open its hard-shelled dinner.
Apparently the bald head that housed the Oresteia
can look, from above, that much like a dimpled rock.
Time has a way of exaggerating things, making myth.
Still, can't you see the cracked skull, the pooling blood?

What Took to the Air

When my mother died, the purple martins
that stepped out of her chest pulled themselves up
into flight, gliding low over the grass

of the campus lawn, foraging the air
for mosquitoes. They waved their dark, arched wings
at me as they passed. And this is the truth.

When dew evaporated from her grave,
it gathered in the clouds, then fell back down
to soak shallow roots that fed the xylem

of the gardenias she loved. That's truth too.
I was there, where flight and a light drizzle
were twin ghosts of the fresh and godless air.

A Sort of Art

They made a sort of music with their feet,
a see-saw slapping as they hit the ground
in time with undead, resurrected years—
the monochrome past of sepia suffering.
They made their music ring in children's ears
all day and night with its staccato beat,
then made the children make another sound,
something like an orchestra for the king
with *mami, papá, dios,* retch, and wail
for notes. It quivered through the king's rich heart.
Now they make another music with bones
crushed and sifted through screens, a whispered trill
that sounds like burning notes. A sort of art
of no remains. Not names. Not even stones.

Earth Shovel

> Look again at that dot. That's here. That's home. That's us . . . a mote
> of dust suspended in a sunbeam . . . the only home we've ever known.
>   —CARL SAGAN, *Pale Blue Dot*

> Drill, baby, drill!
>   —MICHAEL STEELE, 2008 Republican National Convention

Photographed from 28,000 miles away in 1972, Earth had the look
of a marble, or so people said. Eighteen years later, we shot it again,
this time from 3.7 billion miles when *Voyager 1,* still traveling at
40,000 miles per hour, was nearly done with this solar system that
occupies a tiny bit of real estate in the known universe. A *dot*
is what we called it then, *pale* and *blue.* A pinprick that's
difficult to make out against its black backdrop of void. Here
we are, on that dot, waving goodbye to *Voyager 1.* And that's
that, I suppose. Now, 28 years later and five miles from home,
huge earth movers are clawing at the ground at a site that's
being prepped. When we ask what for, no one can tell us.
The sound of the heavy machinery has already become a
curtain of ambient noise dropped over our days. When a mote
of some black substance swirls in the light-gray glass of
water I pour from the sink, I shrug. The porch is covered in dust.
I drive my car by the grace of plants and animals suspended
in the Earth's crust for more than 100 million years, cooked in
a sort of clay pot by pressure and heat. But that's about to be a
chapter of the past. Fifty or sixty years at most. By then a sunbeam
will power our cars and hoverbikes. Or simply fall on our ashes. The
thing about the universe is that it seems infinite, but really it's only
a ceaseless series of extinctions. I think about that on the drive home.
Over 5 billion species have been here. And 99.9% are gone. We've
been here about an hour on Sagan's Cosmic Calendar. Have you ever
thought about that? Last week a guy at the bar said, *I ain't known*
about none of that. All I know's we'll have plenty of oil if we just drill
down deep enough. Today two friends showed me their new baby.
They were happy, as if they expect a world for her. This is not a drill.

....

Anthem

We sang the same song time and time again.
Everybody sang it, warbling off-key,
without betraying anything was wrong.
The parents sang. The children sang along.
We taught a sort of lyric purity.
We put our own stamp on original sin.

There seemed to be a magic in that song,
the same one we sang time and time again.
We worshipped it as if on bended knee,
although we stood each time we sang it. Free
to put our own stamp on original sin,
we watched the others to make sure they sang

with proper respect, proper dignity,
and no deviation among the throng
that freedom song sung time and time again.
Putting our own stamp on original sin,
we sang facing a banner that was hung
in skies so thick with ash we couldn't see.

MMXX

after Larkin

Old men, having cast out their fishing lines,
wait to feel some tension, wait patiently.
They sip beer, say it's good to be outside,
while others gather with signs in the park
beneath oppressive waves of summer sun.
People see each other, but not faces.
There's something else here no one sees at all.
The interrogating song of a lark

overscores the air. From their scrubbed and bleached
houses, children peer through fingered sunblinds
at all the stony statesmen and sovereigns
falling down. They want to join in the play,
topple horsemen, explorers, kings, and queens.
Their parents' screens fill with advertisements
for off-brand tissue, and drunks stalk the pubs.
A decade passes every other day.

Somehow, the biggest issue is caring.
It's hard not to think everything's over
as trucks arrive, tents are set up in fields,
and people in hazmat suits measure lines
while the lark's song punctuates a silence.
Some assure the Lord won't harm His servants,
that the faithful remain safe as houses,
while pardoned liars wave from limousines.

A fish swims in its complete innocence
toward a hooked fly, but spooks at a twitch since
fear is what it knows best. It swims on past.
Not too much luck today, think the old men.

....

In half an hour or so, they'll rise, tidy
up, return to their silent marriages.
The fish drifts back toward the hook, no longer
afraid. Ever such innocence, again.

Isolation

The anole moved from hanging plant
to hanging plant, walking the wire
of the porch screen. He turned his head

to regard me when he paused, flared
his throat like a Japanese fan.
From here, we were too far away

to hear a ventilator's rasp.
Too far to hear a mother's sigh.
We seemed to listen anyway,

still as we were. As still as trees.
He blinked his eyes against the breeze.
He had a hand I couldn't grasp.

Appetite

Emerging from her cocoon without a mouth,
the luna moth climbs onto a stem to unfurl
and dry her wings. She'll find a mate tonight.

There will be no kiss. There will be no taste.
There will be no speech or song. After midnight
the still, silent couple will join like drops of rain.

She'll go her way, and he'll go his, and there
will be no need. Nothing sharp or savory, nothing
bland or sweet. She'll lay two hundred eggs.

Then a final rest on a barn door's hinge, staring
at the lightbulb's perfect yolk. And nothing
like hunger, though hunger's what we feel.

The Son

After the carcass had been hung on a hook,
the boy left the barn, walked back to the house
and past his mother at the sink, then sank

into the sea of his bed. And the angel that sought
the boy was not the angel of his father's world.
The angel found him, moved toward him in silence,

and reached to touch his hand. She spread her wings
to enfold the child and pulled him down into
something like a deep-carved mine below the storm

where a heart could be made whole. The boy drowned
in his gratitude for a salvation he couldn't seek.
At grace, his mother offered her hand for him to hold.

Tongue & Torque

It's getting dark when the detectives find
the tongue of the missing girl in the field,
not far from the spot where they'd found her hair,
her bag, her books, her crucifix, her clothes.

They tag and bag and clock out for the night.
In the trees the bird (is it a swallow
or a nightingale?) watches as it sings
its song about the sameness of the day.

Thus the world works its weightless torque, spinning
nearly one thousand forty miles per hour.
Thus the day ends with a grinding darkness.
The bird's song stops. And then it starts again.

Somewhere down the hill a tongue strikes the wall
of a church bell, and the peal trembles out
into the darkening air. And somewhere else
the sun is rising to the sound of bells.

One moment that bell's tongue meets its thick wall,
and seconds later the sound still shimmers,
resonating in the river's current
and flowing downstream to oblivion.

One moment the workers on a great tower
talk of measurements and tools, grooves and torque,
and the next they're spitting out gibberish,
lips flapping in a confusion of tongues.

The architects of medieval castles
often placed torture chambers beneath stairs
winding underground to muffle the cries
of victims and preserve the dignity

....

of dinner parties and prayers to the Lord
above. The twisting screams would lose their torque,
fall to a whisper in the upper rooms
where priests might place the host upon a tongue.

In the long history of human torture
you read plenty of stomach-turning things,
but of these it's *removal of the tongue*
that always brings the bile up to my throat.

A special tweak for men who cursed the king
or girls who could not be trusted to hold
their tongues in the wake of his appetite.
Dead men don't tell tales. Nor do tongueless girls.

Once a girl asked for a god to see her
before she lost her tongue, before flying
from her body and fluttering away
into the night and into darker myth.

Now Philomela's nearly everywhere,
and so's her senseless song. A swallow's trill
is warbling now in human ears while we
believe we've left our torture far behind.

When I was a child and heard that sometimes
epileptics will swallow their own tongues
during grand mal fits, I asked my mother
how that could be possible. *Well,* she said,

straight-faced, *it's not attached to anything.*
And when I stared, puzzled, moving my tongue
around in my mouth, she just laughed and laughed.
I still don't know if she was teaching me

....

how to be cruel or how to love the lie
you tell a trusting child, to love that power.
A power she never had anywhere else.
Most of the time, she had to bite her tongue.

And now she'll never say another thing
to me or anyone. Robert Frost said
that poetry is that thing that gets lost
in translation, as if one human tongue

can never completely reach another.
But my college French professor told me,
If you really want to learn this language,
the best way is to sleep with a French girl.

I didn't do well with that assignment,
though I did go out with a stateside girl
from that class and did my best to translate
my tongue to hers on our very first date.

Two years on, that translated to marriage,
and two years later to divorce. The world
thus works its torque, circling the sun, spinning
nearly one thousand forty miles per hour.

I don't even know if she's still alive,
if her skull still has a tongue and can sing.
But I do know a bird still sings its song
about the sameness of the day. I know

the same darkness is coming to the night.
And I know somewhere a girl is trying
to push away the tongue of a stranger
or a father in our enlightened world.

....

And in the ME's cold office, a tongue
lies on a metal table, waiting there
for the weightless torque of the world's spinning
to bring its lost skull there so it can sing.

To Sleep

They die so many times before our eyes,
the footage rolling in a loop for hours:
run down or choked or shot or cast in flames.
They disappear as pixels dissipate
into the memory's short-term holding zone,
a wasteland filled with nothing we hold dear—
like oceans where trash and bodies are dumped
or gold-gilt back alleys where love is trumped—
the place we store cries we don't want to hear,
where we see no sin in standing alone.
In sleep, though, the faces regenerate,
and white noise coheres into whispered names.
We know it then, that all their deaths are ours.
We die so many times before we rise.

Brayer

From four fields down this morning, the Walkers' mule
is braying as if he's had enough, as if he'll kick off
the human arms bringing his burden, as if he'll have
no more of those days he works straight through.

Here is a flower. And here is an imperial moth.
Here is a kitten playing with a tennis ball. Here
is the shooter taken without incident. And here
is a child. Here is a congressman calling for prayer.

There goes the Walkers' mule again, unbowing his head,
stretching his muscled neck, and letting out a bray
like a peal of trumpet and kettledrum as if he could make,
by breath or will, yesterday's burden dissolve today.

Pastime

What a strange metaphor, to say that the man
on the mound had *telegraphed his pitch,* the one
the batter just turned into a three-run dinger.

A little more deception with the ball, and that thing
would have been a harmless can of corn. But *telegraph!*
Just picture it: a pitcher tapping a message in code

on a hinged lever, sending it along a wire that runs
from the mound to the plate. What trouble to take
to send a message he doesn't want the batter to receive!

Then again, maybe it's a metaphor not so out of place.
After all, we were already playing ball in the late 1860s,
when telegraphy was the state of the art in communication,

when Union soldiers had just finished kicking the seats
of Confederate pants, when a run was called an *ace,*
you played to the score of twenty-one, some games took days,

and this nation and species and planet still had a chance.

The Beetles

All you need is love, little guy, shiny
beetle, tiny god nestled in your green
carapace. You mirror back my love, you
don't let me down as you crawl all over
every little thing on this planet, all
four hundred thousand of your known species.
Good morning, good morning! Every dawn you're
here, there, and everywhere. When I see you,
I feel fine knowing you're oblivious,
just doing your beetle things. Even when
kicked around by human feet, you dears just
let it be, just carry on, go nowhere
man can reach. And would you believe that I
need you, bug, more than any human soul?
Oh! Darling, it's true. So let me watch you
pace along this sidewalk. Here comes the sun
quietly rising. If in its shine or
rain, I'll just kneel here transfixed. Because there's
something in the way you move that makes the
two of us one world not found across the
universe, what Donne called an *everywhere.*
Voracious little thing, eat up my time.
What else do I need but you, you nearly
xenomorphic gem? Human life is so
yesterday. I believe in you. I'm your
zealot—your hysterical, screaming fan.

Exegesis of Jonah

I like to imagine that one night somewhere
between Joppa and Nineveh, sometime between
the sailors' pitch and the whale's belch, a couple
of young lovers strolled the beach hand in hand

beneath the sun's muted light reflected off the surface
of the moon. I like to imagine them new to each other,
still shy, looking more at the flickering glints on the waves
than at each other's dim face at first. Then some force

draws their lips together. Just look at them there,
in the very spot where spat-out Jonah will later land
like a hurled javelin, kissing as if they could make the world
disappear, kissing until they have to stop, to come up for air,

before returning to their search for something holy there.

The Vault

Kingsolver tells young writers to stop smoking
and obey the posted speed limit—to stay alive
long enough to become wise. Here's more advice, kids:
Don't grab the rail of an open stairwell from a flight
four stories high, bend your knees low, then spring
to hurl your young body over that rail (and the floor

far below) as if you were an arboreal gibbon
sailing routinely from tree to tree, out of curiosity
and a marginal confidence that you'll make it
over the next rail and onto that flight's flat landing.
The fact I made it is beside the point. I still flinch
at the memory of the world in which I didn't.

The Elect

Like the vole, I have wandered a field
under the greater sky, not knowing nine-tenths
of my brethren are already gone.

I have found another of my kind
and joined her walk toward the sun
in its setting. I have entered the earth.

I have nosed the root that feeds the vine.
I have seen the remains of others, stopping
and walking on. One morning I woke,

and the other did not. I have felt the warmth
that dries the dew. I have been happy.
Above me, I have seen a wheeling halo of birds.

I Listened to the Song "I Watched the Film *The Song Remains the Same*"

I think I was in sixth grade that day
that I punched the kid three years younger
than me on a dare from some girls.

No provocation at all. My back was to him,
then I just wheeled around and landed
a few quick ones on his face and chest.

He looked more confused than angry.
The girls congratulated me for my obedience.
So that was a day in elementary school,

which is surely, along with junior high
and high school, one of the worst places
or states of being possible in the seventy years

or so that most of us get, don't you think?
That kid had some problems in his family,
though I can't recall what they were.

That state of being, elementary school,
was probably worse for him than for me.
I don't remember the last time I saw him.

Years later my father told me he'd heard
that this same kid, then in his late teens
or early twenties, when he was arrested

for public intoxication or drug possession
or just hating the whole damn world,
did his best to urinate through the bars

of his holding cell and onto the feet
of the arresting cops. Sometimes,
without trying to, I picture him

trying to get them, but imagine
his weak stream falling short as his curses
dwindle to soft grunts and whispers.

And if I'm not careful, I then see him
dropping to his knees and passing out,
his face hitting the floor, sliding

through his own slick piss straight
into a momentary halo of oblivion.
The imagination is dangerous.

And something of a godlike power,
at least according to Samuel Taylor Coleridge.
He called it *esemplastic,* an obscure

and idiosyncratic term that basically means
having the ability to fuck with damn near everything.
And maybe to set things right. Truth, too,

is dangerous. The knowing of it, that is.
A little learning is a dangerous thing
is a line you know, whether or not you know

Alexander Pope is its author. Its truth
seems self-apparent because just a little knowledge
can make you feel an unearned confidence,

as if you know all you need to know
and now need to know no more, but can take
what you know to build yourself up

and to grind down anyone else you'd like to.
Thus the relationship of most college professors
to their students. But a little knowledge is also dangerous

because it can be a lure to deeper knowledge,
can swallow you as if into a vortex or down,
as the kids say, a rabbit hole, and then you're lost

trying to get to the "bottom of things"
(i.e., all there is to know), and nobody
ever returns from that little adventure.

Because no amount of knowledge ever amounts
to truth. Do you want to know a truth?
John Keats is the greatest poet of this language.

And he said that truth is beauty. And, in fact,
that the inverse is true. So all you really need
are the eyes in your head, if you believe Keats.

Don't hold the fact that he died at twenty-five against him.
That kid knew what he was talking about. True,
he was riffing on some very old paired ideas there.

Delight and instruction, sweetness and light,
beauty and truth. But it's the simplicity of his equation:
beauty *is* truth. *That is all ye need to know.*

....

I love the archaic, almost biblical sound of that *ye*.
It makes the pronouncement sound absolute,
brooks no argument. This truth is true, damn it.

Of course, there's truth, and then there's truth.
That's what got under Plato's skin, why he wanted
to pitch the poets out of his Republic. He knew well

that poetry is an art that's equal parts revelation
and deception. It's true. Just ask Homer. Or Aristotle.
Or anyone who's ever really looked into it.

Poets have to be exquisite liars. And Plato
is not the only one who has a hard time with that.
Some readers, too many, demand a purity of truth.

But some things are more important than truth.
And a lot of things are a lot worse than a lie.
Some other schoolkid is getting hit for nothing

as you read this. And some other children
are being raped by their fathers and uncles and brothers,
some others feeling hunger every second of every day.

There's a song on Sun Kil Moon's *Benji*
called "I Watched the Film *The Song Remains the Same*."
(The album's pure genius, by the way,

though some of Mark's longtime fans
think it's betrayal-level garbage. To hell with them.)
In that song, Mark Kozelek remembers

....

having once been *baited into clocking*
some undeserving boy, as he puts it,
out on the elementary school playground.

And in the song, Mark apologizes to that boy
across the years and untold miles
as if such a thing could ever really be done.

You know it can't. I know it can't.
But in the ten-plus minutes of that song,
amidst the ethereally beautiful finger picking

of Mark's old guitar, it seems not only
like it's possible, but that it's happened.
And you have been its only witness.

Sometimes I tell my students that poetry is
the persistent, futile effort to earn self-forgiveness.
Some roll their eyes. And inside, I'm rolling my eyes

at myself too most of the time, including now,
knowing my penchant for grand pronouncement
gets the best of me more often than not.

But I believe what I tell them. And I'm a god
of futility. Just look at me now, still
writing these lines as you grow suspicious

of the investment you've made in the poem.
Around stanza thirty-three you started to doubt
the veracity of its opening anecdote

after you'd already begun to grow tired
of its self-indulgent, meandering, prosaic style.
But it really happened, reader, though there's nothing

I can do to assure you I'm not abusing your trust.
Still, this prostrate god lays down this next line,
and whether or not you believe it's true I say

the rabbit stretches in the grass, the cockroach
scurries in the walls, the dew resolves
into a gas, the yellow-throated warbler calls,

the sunlight shifts across the leaves, the asp
and mongoose share a dance, the wasps
build nests under the eaves, the stiffened robin

feeds the ants, the moon obliviates its phase,
the water-walking spiders float, and days
and days and days and days are swallowed

nightly in my throat. Could any of that
be something to you? Or set anything right?
Or is it all just dissipating breath?

One of the things I love about *Benji*
is how it strikes an almost perfect balance—
not a calm equilibrium, but a measured dance

of extremes—between profundity and absurdity,
between pathos and bathos, between self-praise
and self-effacement, between sheer solipsism

and an almost pure empathy, as in the line
wherever you are, that poor kid, I'm so sorry.
If you can listen to the way Mark delivers that line

and think he doesn't really care, that this is all
cynical artifice, that he wouldn't give
damn near everything to be able to go back

and make it right, well then, dear reader,
I sure as hell wouldn't want to live in your skin.
But redemption is always possible, so read on.

Another selling point for *Benji* is that,
like all great works of art, it's obsessed with death.
From Mark's cousin Carissa to his truck-driver uncle

to his grandma to his friend Brett to the thirteen victims
of Richard Ramirez to the wife of Jim Wise
to John Bonham to Peter Grant to James Gandolfini

to two people in a Portland mall to twelve people
in a Colorado theater to twenty-one people
in a San Diego McDonald's to fifty kids under the age

of nineteen on an island in Norway to twenty-six
children and adults at an elementary school
once attended by Adam Peter Lanza,

it's as relentless and inescapable as the fact itself.
Who wouldn't want to spend one hour,
one minute, and fifty seconds on it right now?

Louis-Ferdinand Céline said, *No art is possible
without a dance with death.* Wallace Stevens said,
Death is the mother of beauty. And I say

that a tried-and-true prescription for living
what might be called a meaningful life is to say
I'm going to die to the mirror each morning.

I'll admit that the desire to quite forget
what the nightingale has never known is about
as human as it gets, but as Flannery O'Connor says,

*The truth does not change according to our ability
to stomach it emotionally.* And the truth is that wishing
won't make it so. The weariness, the fever, and the fret

are here to stay. Even if we aren't. Hell, even as a species.
If you scale what we know of time down to a calendar year,
everything we call A.D. takes up about four seconds

(see Carl Sagan). From a cosmic perspective,
a human life is as ephemeral as a mayfly's
and just as important. My friend Jake knew

something about ephemerality. He dedicated his life
to a project he called *Inscriptions for Air.* A white boy
from northern Alabama, he set out to write elegies

for every martyr of the Civil Rights Movement
after seeing the forty-one names that are etched
into water-washed stone in Montgomery.

When a forgotten murder or lynching was unearthed
in research, he simply expanded the project.
He called it *the work of a life.* Through four books

he wasn't halfway done with the first forty-one.
But his brain was grand enough to hold it all,
as strong as his heart. Then one December night

he dressed in his characteristically dapper style,
went to a holiday party with his wife, and while there
felt something wrong in his head and left.

He was forty years old. You don't just write some
of the greatest poems of your generation, give
everything of yourself in the interest of everyone else,

put on a tie, button your coat, then go to a party
and die. That just doesn't happen. Until it does.
You don't just go until you do, like breath on wind.

You don't just go to the convenience store for Skittles
in your comfortable hoodie and die until you do.
You don't just reach toward your glove compartment

with a child strapped in the back seat and die
until you do. You don't just go for a run
on a country road or on a late-night run for burgers

and die until you do. You don't just turn out the light
in your own bedroom, go to sleep, and die until you do.
The stiffened robin feeds the ants. And the dew

....

resolves itself into a gas. Days and days and days and days,
you swallow the thought that the terrible, inevitable
impossibilities could be resurrected and reversed.

And each morning you wake wanting a more exquisite lie.
I want Jake to be alive now and writing his poems,
want him to finish *Inscriptions for Air,*

want to see him again, to thank him for what
he's given. And I want to go adopt that rescue dog
that my dying friend Nina had to return,

by herself, when it didn't get along with the dog
her family already had. *I'll take him, Nina,*
I want to say. And while I'm there, I want

to take the cancer from her breast and spine.
And I want to go back to twelve years old
and not let my Chihuahua outside off the leash

so he won't be torn apart in front of me
by my great uncle's collie. And I want to go
to the Oran of Camus's *La Peste* with a gun

and shoot Cottard before he can shoot the street dog.
I know I'm supposed to empathize with that man
in a strange way, to forgive him out of some grand

existential human solidarity, but damn it, Camus—
an innocent dog? Fuck that guy. And since I've got a gun
in this exquisite lie now, I want to go to a white enclave

in Florida and shoot a man in the back of the head
before he can approach a seventeen-year-old
with Skittles in the pocket of his hoodie.

And I want to find that kid from elementary school
and apologize for those undeserved punches
from forty years ago. So when I listen to the song,

"I Watched the Film *The Song Remains the Same*,"
if I'm not careful I begin to think that making things right
is possible as I feel the slow, ephemeral breath

drift in and out of my lungs like Mark's fingers
floating across the strings of that old guitar.
A rabbit stretches in the grass. A warbler calls.

Halfway through the labyrinthine drafting
of this poem, I remembered the kid's name.
The imagination is dangerous. So is the internet.

There's a photograph in the online obituary I found,
and I recognized his face at once. (Is it one detail too far
if I tell you he was forty-nine?) It gives no cause of death.

Sometimes loved ones would just rather not say.

The Ghost

In the beginning you were surely there
for everyone to see—some sentinels,
a truant scholar, your own suicidal son
wandering through the fog. No one

had a doubt. Later it was harder to be sure
when you only showed yourself to the boy
and all you said had already been said
and the mother just gaped at empty space.

In the end you turned out to be as white
as bone. You were there if *there* was the ground.
And above it there was nothing anymore
but haunted memories for our basest use.

.

As Though Nothing Was Wrong

Listen to the silence, let it ring on.
—IAN CURTIS

Let's calculate the odds that human life
will last another ten or hundred years,
then turn the tables upside down and dance
to patterned pulses from a neutron star.
Let's dance along the edge of a thin knife,
flailing our arms while staring through our tears,
and learn what is and isn't permanence,
how much we can take, exactly how far
we can go till desperation takes hold.
Let's map our steps by digital design,
then twist as if we're dangling from a hook.
Let's oscillate between whisper and shout,
between collapsing and walking in line,
and dance to the silence day in, day out.

See Here It Is—

I held out my hand above a small bed
in Rome and tried to feel another hand—
living, skeletal—held up to touch mine.

I tried to see my face's reflection
in the pane above a death mask and felt
a stillness in the air, felt nothing there.

From the Steps below chatter and laughter
from young, healthy lungs rose through the window,
and the chirps of phones sounded like birdsong.

Plaster nightingales kept silent vigil,
perched atop mantels and display cases.
They still stared blankly as I turned to leave.

I bought a shirt, then took a train to see
the stone. At the cemetery's gateway
a sentinel lay in perfect stillness—

a gray striped tabby, one front paw stretched out
across a guidebook, one back hanging off
the table's edge, closed eyes oblivious.

I followed the path that paw pointed to,
treading pebbles that shifted under foot,
till I stood before it. *See here it is—*

I knelt, stretched out my hand to touch etched stone,
and felt a grand, empty bewilderment.
Then, down deep, something like satisfaction.

Two hundred years too late, I found nothing
I'd waited for. My wife was there with me
the whole time. And, reader, she's with me still.

Still. That word's like a bell. It even rhymes
slant with *bell,* echoes the echoes of odes
and the voice of Ian Curtis. Listen.

Do you hear that, reader? Nothing's coming
here. As it had there, certain as a bell.
As certain as a song that stays the same.

As certain as a stone in the shadow
of a pyramid, certain as nothing
being certain. Keats said he was certain

of only two things: one, *the holiness
of the heart's affections,* and two, *the truth
of imagination.* I'm certain too

of only two things: how a long-dead hand
can still reach out to craft a living soul
and help it feel the heft of days that flow

through life like water through outstretched fingers,
and how my wife and I were there that day
standing above the silence of a tomb

and still—strange, small miracle—we are here.

Finishing Listening to "Finishing Jubilee Street"

Every time I've made something that I've thought
might last, might stand outside myself, might live
at least a while after I'm in the ground,
I've risen, pumped a fist, and then fallen

into bed, slept like a lotus eater,
and awakened to a world of strange light,
as if reentering a life I thought
I'd left behind. Everything still to do.

Everything still to do today, to do
tomorrow, to do some time later on.
The best poem always the poem unwritten.
This morning I'm thinking about that year

when I smoked thirty cigarettes a day
and boasted it was a slow suicide
to anybody who cared to listen.
I was nineteen years old. If I'd been Keats,

I'd have had six years left. Now fifty-six,
I'd like another fifty-seven, please.
Or at least enough to make something right
or good or worth redeeming all the wrong.

Not that I've been guilty of too much wrong.
Like Hamlet, I'd measure myself to be
indifferent honest, but also like him
I could accuse myself of everything.

....

And so I spend most days trying to earn
self-forgiveness. (Futile, but relentless.)
I start with prayers to lords of other worlds
I conjure through a stubborn act of will.

I lie myself into another life—
momentary, but made—and wander there,
trying to find something that means something
in the heart of a man I've never been.

I've never been the son standing in jail
with his mother as they both hear the news
of the father's death, the surrounding cops
chuckling. I've never been the father

learning that his son has stepped off a cliff
after dropping acid and fallen straight
to his death at fifteen. I've never been
a junkie, except for those cigarettes

and maybe for the high of making poems.
I've never been Keats, certain of the truth
of the imagination and his heart.
I've only been certain of my own death.

Still, I always try to make something else.
There's a perfect song called "Jubilee Street"
on Nick Cave's album *Push the Sky Away*.
No matter how many times I listen

I can't figure out how it progresses
to that stunning crescendo from its slow,
drawling start. And I'd guess Nick can't either.
Three tracks later there's another song called

....

"Finishing Jubilee Street," and in it
he talks of falling into a deep sleep
and then waking in a panic, searching
for the beautiful young bride of his dream.

The best song always the song unwritten,
always a ghost drifting beyond your reach,
hiding all away until unbidden.
Everything to do. Everything to do.

If I could have seen The Birthday Party
play live in 1983—that year
when I inhaled scores of carcinogens
two hundred times a day—I'm pretty sure

my hand would have shot up when Nick Cave lurched
into "Sonny's Burning" with a question.
But today, thirty-seven years later,
even Nick does not, I think, want to die.

And as I said above, I'd rather not
myself. So if the lord of this world won't,
I'll pray that the lord of another one
might give me a bit more time to live there

in its dream, cursing a father, pulling
a mother out of a conjurer's hat,
reanimating a torn-apart dog,
and inhaling a pure, innocent air.

Maybe there I will make something that lasts.
I'll fall into bed if I do, sleep hard,
and wake to the miracle of these dogs
and my wife—and her red, red hair, O lord—

....

all of this coming down into a life
too good for any man, where everything
is still to be done, this strange paradise
where I'd rather not finish anything.

Final Visitation

After talking with him for thirty minutes
as he lay cocooned in a thin wool blanket,
I told my father I had to head back to Conway.

He turned his ashen face a bit and said, *Conway . . .*
that's where my son lives. I met my sister's eyes
before fixing his in mine to say, *Father, I am your son.*

His eyes widened in that way that makes
us say, *You look like you've seen a ghost,*
or as if he'd found himself the quarry of a hunt.

I touched his hand before I left to show him
I was real. I think I could have walked through walls
to get to my car, so grateful was I to be that ghost.

Here, Where Men Sit

As I dangle my legs over the gorge,
I remember the time we came to class
to find Mr. Dickey seated alone

at the head of the long workshop table,
a hint of yellow blooming on his skin.
We took our seats in silence, matching his.

Minutes later, Deborah was at the door.
Please, Jim, go to the hospital. He did,
slowly pulling himself up from the chair

and then more slowly walking between us—
we'd stood, offered help—reaching out to touch
a shoulder or arm as he stepped into

the ending of his life. I sometimes think
of him sitting in the classroom that day
when someone says the word *resignation*.

It was as if he'd sat down in that chair
with no intention of standing back up.
As I swing my legs over the canyon,

I think of Keats sitting with his brother
as Tom's consumption takes its hold, wiping
blood from his brother's lips and breathing in,

almost certainly, his own early death,
and I think of Hardy sitting alone
in a pew late in life beneath the eyes

of his mute, purblind Doomsters far above.
As I swing my legs over the abyss,
I remember my father in his chair

in the living room watching cable news,
reclined and wishing death upon a child.
And I remember sitting with my wife

as they rolled his casket back down the aisle.
As I sit here trying to write this poem,
swinging my legs over my own dark void,

I fall deep into that recurrent dream
of finding my long-dead mother sitting
on the top brick step leading to the porch,

looking out over a large, empty field.
I step out through the front door and sit down
beside her, and we just stare straight ahead.

I don't know if I'm providing comfort
or adding to her pain. The only thing
I'm sure of is that we're both exhausted

and that sitting there feels something like rest.

The Passing Train

The train to nowhere blares its absurd horn,
and seraphim scamper off the tracks,
a few even fluttering into flight.

From the windows, children stare like monkeys
from a grim researcher's cage. Their parents
gaze deep into their small, iridescent boxes

with a glistening film on their eyes. One little girl
sings the song she's been taught, but no one
seems to hear except for one fiery seraph

who drifts back down through a cloud of flaked rust
in the caboose's windy wake and listens hard
until the last notes are wholly, wholly, wholly gone.

Inscription in the Wake

for Samuel Hammond, Delano Middleton, and Henry Smith, killed by South Carolina Highway Patrol officers in Orangeburg, SC, on February 8, 1968

and after Jake Adam York

Clio says there's a missile coming that's washed itself clean
      through the air and through the years with its spiraling flight,
that's spun through windows and windshields and backs,
      over battlefields and balustrades and grassy campus hills,
a missile made from manacles and from manumission,
      a missile made of other missiles that are sometimes called
bullets and buckshot and bowling balls, one spiraling on
      and carrying them all, washing them all clean in its spinning,
leaving everything and nothing in its wake, everybody
      and nobody, every body and no body, every cry and silence
in the fire-enlightened night. Clio says it's coming now,
      but nobody can hear. She says something was coming then,
but nobody could hear, says something has been written
      and thus nothing was written then, and what's been written
says the outsider is there and thus he is not sequestered
      in an upper room, that he's there and is waving his arms
like a conductor to make whistles be heard and to make
      missiles fly, there to be an outsider who can be cast out,
to be the outcast heaped with a town's guilt to carry out
      a plan that no one can put into the air along with the missile
and its self-cleansing flight. And Clio says whether or not
      missiles flew through that night or through the night before
from across fields and across a century that missiles still flew
      through that night because the saying of it was in the air
and so stays in the air even as it's written down on white paper
      and locked in the vault of white imagination that some call
history. But the one missile that's coming, that's always
      coming, that washes itself clean with its endless spiraling flight,

....

is the missile that found Henry's neck and Samuel's back
and Delano's heart, that passed through body and soul
and inscribed three names on the air in whispered breath
and mothers' cries and chiseled three names into granite
lying below its flight, its flight that's still coming even now
and has been coming through the years and through the lives
of Trayvon and Michael and Tamir and Alton and Philando
and Stephon and Atatiana and Breonna and Ahmaud and Rayshard
and washing itself clean each time with its relentless spiraling
through years and imagination and fears and denial and power,
and we all know it's coming now. And Clio says that a muse
can never hold a pen, that what's written is always what's written
in someone else's hand. I see, and I can hear. And when I hear
Clio say *Take up your lyres,* I think I hear *Take down your liars,*
and I look at my hands and look at my skin and look at my face
and see in the mirror that I am someone else. A missile is still
coming here. You know that it's coming now, the same missile
that found Henry's neck and Samuel's back and Delano's heart
in the town where I was born and never knew. A missile in motion
stays in motion as long as it's in a void. *What do you hear and what
do you see? What is in your hands?* What if a pen in hand could be
a kind of rake that could sift through what's left in the widening wake
of the missile's endless flight? What if it could gather the blood
and bone and dirt and fire and ash and voice that were shed
and mix all that into an ink with which you might inscribe
what's still whispering in the air? What's still coming.

What Nothing Was

for the MV Alta, *October 2018 to February 2020*

Some well-meaning people told me that to find peace
of mind I should try to think about the sound
a tree might make (or not) if it fell in a forest

when there was no one around to hear.
I thought about the ears of squirrels and bears
and owls, and about the minds of human beings.

Then I thought about a disabled, abandoned,
nearly forgotten cargo ship floating
atop three hundred million cubic kilometers

of ocean for sixteen months. Like a leaf
falling from a Siberian aspen, did it drift
in almost complete silence out of view

of every human eye? I like to think of you,
MV *Alta,* out there alone, sloughing off
fine flakes of orange rust from your bow

into the heavier waves, the wire ropes
stretched from your crane becoming a sort of lyre
making the faintest whistle in the northern wind.

I like to think of the Greenland sharks,
of the humpback whales, of the pollock,
cod, mackerel, halibut, and haddock

that swam beneath your hull. I like to think
of the sooty tern and the wandering albatross
regarding you from above with curious eyes.

....

And I like to think of the shadows of clouds
drifting across your deck on calmer days
before a storm pushed you onto the rocky Irish coast.

All that time so far, far, far from all of us.

Stony Sleep

In the end we made a pillow for our heads
from broken brick and twisted rebar.
We huddled together in the waning sunlight
and pulled a blanket of ash up to our chins.
We nestled close, squeezed out all air between us,
and even then, wound like a ball of snakes,
we felt our warmth begin to drain. In the shadows
of reeling indignant desert drones,
we felt the molten rock embrace our feet.
Cradled now, we sleep the sleep of stones.
Maybe in twenty centuries you'll find us here,
another fetal xenolith waiting to be reborn.

On Listening to "Atmosphere" One More Time

After all the years of my obsession
with every note and every word,
with the bass and synth and drums
and sweep of chimes, with the video
in grainy black and white filled
with stills amid a funereal procession,
today all I can think of is Candy
and how the people who took her in
shortly before Ian died must have,
surely, surely must have, had to have,
could not not have shown her that love
that makes it worth being torn apart.

Suspense

The woolly mammoth lumbered over bones
of dinosaurs and crocodiles and men,
and then was gone. The children of Pompeii
were buried under pyroclastic flow.
Now we've made enough bombs to vaporize
all nations, races, and religious sects.
Still time flows forward while amber suspends.

On an Italian shelf, silent as stones,
two mites and a fly, Triassic insects
trapped in amber for two hundred million
years, hold history's most bated breath today.
For eons now they've been dying to know.
They stare with tiny prehistoric eyes,
just itching to see how this damned thing ends.

ACKNOWLEDGMENTS

Thank you to the editors of the publications in which the following poems, some in different forms, first appeared:

32 Poems: "The Elect," "The Fall of a Turtle," "Pastime," and "Suspense"; *Birmingham Poetry Review:* "Isolation"; *Cave Wall:* "To Sleep"; *Cincinnati Review:* "Earth Shovel"; *The Common:* "Appetite"; *Copper Nickel:* "The Servant's Ear"; *Crazyhorse:* "*As Though Nothing Was Wrong*"; *Four Way Review:* "The Beetles"; *The Greensboro Review:* "Brayer" and "A Sort of Art"; *Harpur Palate:* "The Son"; *Italian Americana:* "*See Here It Is—*"; *New Ohio Review:* "Final Visitation"; *Nimrod International:* "Inscription in the Wake" and "Tongue & Torque"; *On the Seawall:* "MMXX"; *Poetry Northwest:* "What Took to the Air"; *River Styx:* "The Vault"; *South Carolina Review:* "*Here, Where Men Sit*"; *Southern Indiana Review:* "Anthem"; *Southern Review:* "Finishing Listening to 'Finishing Jubilee Street'" and "Kick in the Jaw"; *storySouth:* "I Listened to the Song 'I Watched the Film *The Song Remains the Same*'" and "What Nothing Was"; *Twelve Mile Review:* "The Ghost"; *Whale Road Review:* "The Father" (as "Night Gardener").

"Anthem," "Brayer," "Earth Shovel," "The Ghost," "Kick in the Jaw," "A Sort of Art," and "To Sleep" were featured on *Verse Daily* (www.versedaily.org).

"*As Though Nothing Was Wrong*," "A Sort of Art," and "To Sleep" also appear in the limited-edition chapbook, *Of Air and Earth* (2019).

....

"Anthem," "Brayer," "Earth Shovel," "MMXX," and "What Nothing Was" also appear in the limited-edition chapbook, *Circa MMXX* (2022).

I am grateful to the Berkshire Taconic Community Foundation and the Amy Clampitt Fund for the support of a residency fellowship at the Amy Clampitt House in Lenox, Massachusetts, in the fall of 2020, where many of these poems were written. Thank you also to the Bread Loaf Writers' Conference, Coastal Carolina University, the Hambidge Center for Creative Arts and Sciences, the Sewanee Writers' Conference, the South Carolina Arts Commission, and the Virginia Center for the Creative Arts for grants, fellowships, and scholarships that have supported my work.

Thank you to my teachers: Fred Chappell, James Dickey, Stuart Dischell, Christine Garren, Alan Shapiro, and Natasha Trethewey. This book would not exist without you.

Thank you to Leigh Anne Couch and Wyatt Prunty for selecting this book for the Sewanee Poetry Series, and to James Long, Barbara Bourgoyne, and the entire editorial and production team at LSU Press.

These poets and editors have given me great support and encouragement, and I am immensely grateful: Terry Kennedy, Jake Adam York, Doug Van Gundy, Andrew Saulters, Rhett Iseman Trull, Katrina Vandenberg, Jon Tribble, Allison Joseph, Edward Hirsch, Rodney Jones, George David Clark, Patrick Phillips, January Gill O'Neil, Chad Davidson, Greg Fraser, Jessica Faust, Ross White, Richard Bausch, and Janine Certo.

Special thanks to Lisa Ampleman and Leigh Anne Couch for careful readings of the manuscript and helpful suggestions for revision.

My deepest gratitude to Holley Tankersley, who was with me in Rome on June 5, 2019, at the grave of John Keats and who—strange, small miracle—is with me still. Thank you for this abiding happiness.

NOTES

"The Servant's Ear": All four gospels of the New Testament report that one of Jesus's disciples took a sword and cut off an ear of one of the arresting priests' servants in Gethsemane, but only Luke tells of Jesus miraculously replacing the severed ear back onto the servant's head.

"The Fall of a Turtle": The strange, apocryphal story of Aeschylus's manner of death can be found in the writings of first-century Latin writer Valerius Maximus.

"A Sort of Art": In 2017, officials from the US Immigrations and Customs Enforcement agency (ICE) sought approval from the National Archives and Records Administration to destroy its records related to sexual abuse and deaths of detainees earlier than the then-current law allowed. In 2018, Propublica released an audio recording of detained immigrant children crying and calling out "Mami" and "Papá" repeatedly while an ICE official is heard joking, "Well, we have an orchestra here."

"MMXX": The poem's end words echo those of Philip Larkin's "MCMXIV."

"The Beetles": Scientists estimate that there are 560 million beetles for every human on Earth. Factoring conservatively for average insect weight, if a person's share of beetles were to sit upon them all at once, that person would be squashed under more than 8 million pounds of pressure. Also, the titles of seventeen Beatles songs appear in the poem.

"The Vault": In a 2008 commencement address at Duke University, Barbara Kingsolver said, "Honestly, it is harrowing for me to try to teach 20-year-old students, who earnestly want to improve their writing. The best I can think to tell them is: Quit smoking, and observe posted speed limits. This will improve your odds of getting old enough to be wise."

"*As Though Nothing Was Wrong*": The poem's title and epigraph are phrases from the lyrics of "Transmission" by Joy Division. The poem makes allusion to this and several other Joy Division songs.

"*See Here It Is—*": The poem's title is a phrase from a late fragment by John Keats, often reprinted under the title "This Living Hand."

"Finishing Listening to 'Finishing Jubilee Street'": The poem's epigraph is the opening exclamation of "Sonny's Burning" by The Birthday Party. The poem makes passing allusion to a number of songs written by Nick Cave, as well as to biographical details of that artist's life.

"*Here, Where Men Sit*": The poem's title is a phrase from John Keats's "Ode to a Nightingale."

"Inscription in the Wake": For details about the 1968 Orangeburg massacre, I am indebted to Jack Shuler's *Blood & Bone: Truth and Reconciliation in a Southern Town* (University of South Carolina Press, 2012). The poem is my attempt to elegize and honor the memory of the victims of that massacre, as well as my attempt to contribute to *Inscriptions for Air,* the unfinished project of the late Jake Adam York. Thank you to the late Jon Tribble, Jake's editor, for encouraging poets to continue Jake's project and vision.

"What Nothing Was": The cargo ship MV *Alta* was disabled and abandoned in October 2018. The ship spent the next sixteen months drifting crewless in the Atlantic Ocean before running aground on the coast of Ireland on February 16, 2020.

"On Listening to 'Atmosphere' One More Time": The poem makes reference to the song "Atmosphere" by Joy Division, originally released in March 1980.

Joy Division's lead singer, Ian Curtis, had a border collie that he named Candy after the Velvet Underground song "Candy Says." In the spring of 1980, Ian's wife Deborah, facing financial pressures and a lack of help while she and her husband were estranged, decided to give Candy away to another family. On May 18, 1980—on the eve of Joy Division's departure for their first American tour—Ian Curtis hanged himself at the age of twenty-three.

Printed in the USA
CPSIA information can be obtained
at www.ICGtesting.com
CBHW031645160924
14306CB00017B/90

9 780807 182543

"*Candy* is a jawbreaker: impossible to swallow but a pleasure to savor. In its layers are the flavors of Pope, Keats, Frost, Sagan, Joy Division's Ian Curtis, but it is Dan Albergotti's astonishing formal acumen, wit, and engagement with sound that make his examination of mortality and the complexities of forgiveness so sweet." —ROSS WHITE

"Albergotti is one of the best practitioners of the most musical branch of contemporary poetry. His poems always rely heavily on, and use to the fullest advantage, a musician's ear for the phrase, the line, the stanza, and the close. This is the most accomplished book yet by one of my favorite poets to read." —CHAD DAVIDSON

"In *Candy,* Albergotti crafts astute and thoughtful meditations on the imperfectness of life, language, and time, while skillfully displaying his natural ability to breathe new energy into established forms, including the sonnet and the abecedarian. From purple martins to *Voyager 1* to beetles (and The Beatles) and Joy Division, Albergotti gives us poems that both challenge and delight." —JANUARY GILL O'NEIL

"Albergotti sees into things, both darkness and light together, without the slightest quaver, and he does so with unfailing grace. Even the most brooding passages here give forth the strong sense of an acute mind and sensibility at play with the possible shapes of words in concert. The music in these poems—both alluded to and actually present in the lines—impressed me greatly. This is poetry of the highest order." —RICHARD BAUSCH

DAN ALBERGOTTI is the author of *The Boatloads* and *Millennial Teeth*. His poems have appeared in many literary journals and have been reprinted in *Best American Poetry* and *Pushcart Prize* anthologies. He lives in Tampa, Florida.

SEWANEE POETRY
Wyatt Prunty and Leigh Anne Couch, Series Editors

LSU PRESS
BATON ROUGE 70803 • lsupress.org

Cover photograph courtesy AdobeStock/Kacpura
Cover design by Barbara Bourgoyne

ISBN 978-0-8071-8254-3

90000 >

9 780807 182543